The Carfacts of DATING!

The Woman's Man-U-Will or Won't Date Guide to Dating

JOY E. CROMETY

ISBN 978-1-956696-08-0 (paperback)
ISBN 978-1-956696-09-7 (hardcover)
ISBN 978-1-956696-10-3 (digital)

Copyright © 2021 by Joy E. Cromety

All rights reserved. No part of this publication may be reproduced, distributed, or transmitted in any form or by any means, including photocopying, recording, or other electronic or mechanical methods without the prior written permission of the publisher. For permission requests, solicit the publisher via the address below.

Rushmore Press LLC
1 800 460 9188
www.rushmorepress.com

Printed in the United States of America

CONTENTS

1. Dating 101 1
2. Check Your Credit Report 10
3. The Value Reality 17
4. Let's Go Shopping
   Get the Carfax 24
5. Concept and Expectations 32
6. Buying for Convenience
   The Hooptie 39
7. Rideshare
   The Uber Driver 42
8. For the Short Term
   The Rental 45
9. Long-Term Option
   The Lease 48

Final Thoughts 55

1
DATING 101

In today's dating market, with all the apps and websites you can visit, it's confusing to say the least about the dating scene and how to properly go about finding what you want out of your dating experience. Understanding what dating is and is not for starters is the first step in the right direction for anyone who wants to be successful at dating and finding the mate they want.

Dating is the romantic stage in relationships whereby two people meet socially with the aim of each assessing the other's suitability as a prospective partner in an intimate relationship or marriage. The result of dating could end in four possible scenarios; friendship, different levels of an intimate relationship, marriage or nothing at all. If you understand the probability that 25% your dating experiences could result in one of four ways, then yes, you have grasped the basics of what dating is.

Dating is also defined as being involved with someone for a period of time. The difference between dating and being in a relationship is the *conversation* (notice I didn't say *understanding*) that two individuals have in regards to the level of mutual commitment you both have agreed upon. Never assume anything in dating. *Always* ask the so-called obvious questions about where your interactions with each other could be heading and have them define it in their words so you understand what it means to them. That's where understandings can get, well, misunderstood. Just because you've been seeing someone for a few months doesn't mean that you're in a relationship with them unless you both agree to it.

There is *no commitment* in dating, unless it is discussed and agreed upon; and dating doesn't imply having sex with that person. So dating multiple men is not only acceptable but is your best opportunity in finding the right one. I know some women will read this and think I'm saying "be a hoe" and start passing judgement on me and anyone who takes this advice. Well, according to the Urban Dictionary, a *Hoe* is defined as "a woman who sleeps with multiple men." So by the basic definition of the word, *any woman* who isn't with the first man that they ever slept with is a Hoe! It doesn't specify a time period like in the same day or month or even weeks—simply that she has slept with multiple men. So guess what, ladies? You're a Hoe, get over it!

Many women will say they aren't hoes by their interpretation of the definition and that it only applies to promiscuous women and not to a woman who has been married more than once, women who've had three boyfriends in the last four years, or women who've had two boyfriends in the same year because one was abusive. Anyone can find a reason not to be placed in this category. Who would want to? People don't have a right to judge, but they will!

Other women prefer to think that by getting something out of the deal doesn't label them as a hoe, but it does by definition make them a prostitute. A *prostitute* according to the Urban Dictionary is a woman with an over exaggerated sense of self-worth who will only date professional men. Usually these gold diggers have nothing special to offer these men beyond vagina and a potential unwanted paternity situation; a female available for companionship in exchange for payment.

So no matter what you choose to do with yourself and your life, someone else will be the one to label and judge you, regardless of how you think you should be perceived. So do what makes you happy!

Understand that your life is yours and your level of comfort with yourself is what *you* determine it to be, not others or society. You can learn to live your life on your own terms, in your own way, and at a pace you choose. Keep in mind that any decision you make that isn't the norm *will* be criticized by others. You have to develop thick skin if you want to live your life freely on your own terms. Also, know that regardless of your choices, if whoever is passing judgement on your life and situation chooses to label you negatively, that's about them and not you.

People's perception of you is based on where they are in the relationship with themselves and what they would do in your situation. That doesn't necessarily make it correct. Therefore, that's not your business. You can't control what people think about you or let their limitations of themselves make you choose a path not designed for you. Opinions are like assholes—everyone has one. Worry about yours. Now, back to your regularly scheduled reading.

Most women have a pretty standard mindset of how they think dating should go. This mindset was passed down from generation to generation. The problem is their mindset has not evolved like the dating world has. A woman's mindset is her hamartia of dating. Years ago, dating consisted mostly of a courting period and arrangements of marriages. Women were taught to be submissive and act ladylike (according to men) in order to receive the coveted goal of becoming some man's wife. (Which was necessary for survival back then!)

This concept still resonates with a lot of women, and the issue is, it's becoming harder and harder to find the elusive husband so many women are searching for. Regardless of how much they do and what advice their grandma and mother gave them for how they attracted men back in their days, they can't seem to find or keep a man. Hence, most single women are unhappy with their dating lives. Many women try to incorporate what they've learned without truly working on themselves first and learning what they really want. Some women are effective at reaching their goals, while others are still in search of the right strategy that will work for them.

This book offers another strategy to understanding dating and learning how to (1) find out what you want and (2) take back control of your dating experience. This is just another strategy and not for everyone because everyone is at a different point in their lives and requires a strategy for where they are. This will give you the flexibility to not only choose your strategy for dating but also the versatility to be able to freely move through each strategy as it suits your needs to maximize your dating experience. So if you're not happy with your dating life, change it to one that does!

The hardest part about understanding dating is changing your mindset about dating. We have all grown up with a belief system and people in our lives forcing us to do, be, and act like what they believe is in our best interest and what will put us in the best light of others. Rarely do you have people in your life who will allow you to develop who you are without trying to make you into someone else. We see this in parents when they encourage girls to act ladylike and not do anything that would make them not look like "their kind of woman" and likewise for raising boys to be their "type of man." Then you wonder why people are confused about who they are.

If we simply let them be who they are and not categorize them as acting like someone else, there would be no need for any kinds of labels. But we have a need to label things out of fear so it makes sense to us, instead of letting people be who they are—which is simply a human being. We were all created differently for a reason. We are supposed to be individuals, not copies of others.

Reprogramming your mind to think for yourself is hard. You have to fight through all your childhood and early adulthood, flawed and unresearched, thinking to find out what it is that you really want and who you truly are.

Many of us don't know who we are. We mimic the people around us or take our cues from social media about who we should be, what our relationship goals should be, what we should wear, and where we should go. These suggestions can help you weed through or give you some idea of what you may like or even what you don't. Remember, though, ultimately, *you* need to decide for *you*! Not knowing who you are is the first mistake in trying to date anyone! "To thine own self be true," as the saying goes. This will be discussed later in the book.

You are allowed to not look like or act like other people. You are allowed to want differently from what others want. You are uniquely you, and your relationships should look uniquely like you also. There will be some similarities in what your relationship will look like, but it should encompass who you are and what you both want from it.

Still think you want to date? Before you continue reading, free your mind from any preconceived notions about dating and allow yourself to simply be introduced to a few new ideas on how to date for what your needs are and where you are in your life's journey. These concepts won't fit or be agreed upon by everyone, and that's fine—it shouldn't—because this isn't one size fits all. These concepts are for someone reading this book. Find one or more that resonates with you and become successful in your dating experiences. You have the control to get the dating life you desire.

In my car-buying experience, I have bought cars, rented cars, and used other forms of transportation. I have realized that I wasn't shopping for cars effectively, and therefore, I didn't get the best possible deal for myself. As I reflected on what I failed to do in my car-buying experience, it registered to me that my thinking process was flawed. I received what I prepared for—to get what *they* wanted me to have and not what *I* wanted. I had to change my approach to car buying, just like I had to change my approach in dating to get the best possible outcome for me! It all starts in the mind.

Some women have experienced all types of dating situations, and others, just a few. Each situation comes with different requirements for mastering and using it. Based on what you are looking for and what you can afford will determine which option works best for you. You will find that it's not the physical (able to provide comfort, emotional support, and sex) that is causing you not to reach your dating goals but your mindset.

Dating in the woman's mindset and not from a male's perspective can leave you with many disadvantages. For one, you may be operating in a manner that will push men away from you. Also, by not changing and sticking to that mindset will be your hamartia (fatal flaw) in dating. Secondly, focusing solely on you or mainly on what you want and need and not on his wants and needs will trigger him into viewing you differently or in some other capacity other than as a wife, which is generally the end goal. This is evident, if you find yourself constantly dating and your relationship goals aren't being met. There is such a thing as "happy spouse, happy house." A partnership goes both ways—it's not all about you.

Men who are successful with women pay attention to and understand a woman's mindset, and therefore, it makes their outcomes with women more predictable. That's why the men (also known as f*ck-boys) who play women are so successful at getting what they want. They read the manual and play you step by step, like clockwork. And you wonder how it could have happened to you.

You want to gather as much information on the subject as possible and search through to find out what you want from it and how to apply what you've learned to make your goals a reality. Being able to comprehend this aspect of dating and understanding what it is and is not will give you the best options to decide what you are looking for in your car buying (dating) experience (i.e., buying for the life of the car, buying for convenience, rentals, lease, or rideshares [these are explained later]). Go into the dating experience with a win-win attitude, no matter what. Want to know why? Read on.

2

CHECK YOUR CREDIT REPORT

As with any car-buying experience, you should first know what you can afford and your creditworthiness. This same rule should also apply in your experiences in dating. Like any place where you will be making a substantial purchase, they will pull your credit report to see what you qualify for. Let's look at your credit report and assess your "dating worthiness."

Basic things being looked at in your credit report is your History, Debt-to-Income Ratio, Hard and Soft Inquiries, and ways to improve your credit score. These areas should be checked to determine whether or not you are eligible to be dating in the first place and how you should be dating.

History gives a picture of how you came to be at the point you are in your dating life—essentially, your struggles and your triumphs. Your history will also give insight into your mindset and will show the health of areas of your emotional and psychological well-being.

Understanding that sharing this information with a potential mate may expose areas that you weren't aware of that are holding you back or may be looked at negatively. Your history is very important, and this is where the assessment should begin. Prospective buyers (suitors) may ascertain things about you such as how long you've been looking for a new/used car (single and why), if you've ever been in any accidents (how damaged are you and whether or not the damage has been repaired), any repos (ever cheated or are you loyal), or if you pay your bills on time (are you reliable and responsible with your life?). All these things will help define your wellness and "dateability" when you explain your status to a potential buyer in terms of where you are with these things and show that they won't be a hindrance to your growth as a person.

This next area is just as important— if not more—than your history because this is the area in which shows how introspective you are and what steps you took to correct issues from your past to become a better person. This is your Debt-to-Income Ratio (Baggage-to-Healing Ratio). If your baggage-to-healing ratio is high, it will lower your dating worthiness, and this makes you a less viable candidate to be in a healthy relationship. So regardless of how beautiful you are, if you have your own house, own a car, pay your own bills, and have everything going for yourself, you may find that men still won't see you as a wife or as girlfriend material.

Most people dating are looking for someone with whom they can build and may be able to deal with you having some baggage; however, too much baggage can be overwhelming. You have to do the work to repair the baggage that is causing you to be in a dysfunctional or unhealthy relationship. You may think that you are healed from a thing until you find yourself holding someone new hostage to a situation that they themselves didn't create in you.

When you lower this ratio (less baggage, more healing), it allows you to be ready to be in a healthy relationship with others. Everyone has baggage, but if your actions—i.e., insecurity, violating someone's privacy, trust issues, daddy or mommy issues, ex issues, or anything that is keeping you from moving forward, it will be viewed negatively to anyone looking to invest in you. So do the work on yourself to address the issues in your life that are adversely affecting your relationship with others and not just in your romantic relationships. Learn to deal with issues as they arise instead of shelving them for never.

Baggage is like wounds. Some are old and so damaged that they need to be reopened and the scar tissue removed before it can heal. It's painful but necessary. Some wounds heal and leave scars. They are no longer painful, they are reminders of what you went through and don't stop you from living your life. They sometimes make you stronger. Some wounds (baggage) are fresh and if tended to in a timely manner properly, can be repaired with barely a mark left. Some people use them as scabs and keep ripping it off to remind them of the pain and never giving it a chance to properly heal. Whatever your wound is, do the work to appreciate the scars and find the beauty in you.

Hard and Soft Inquiries are those inquiries about your past relationships with others. Only the person receiving the information will determine the impact it has on their judgment of you. Hard inquiries are what is being looked at for major situations like moving in together, commitment, and marriage. Soft inquiries are used to see if there are enough interesting things about you to want to spend more time together and perhaps date.

Hard inquiries can cover how you are with your exes, people you've dated, and/or those with whom you have had sex. (I wouldn't recommend answering this one.) It can also include asking about sexually transmitted infections (STIs), fetishes, how you handle your finances, ambitions, and anything that can be a red flag to further things in a relationship with others. Use your discretion when revealing this information until you feel the dating is moving forward toward something you want to invest your time in before disclosing some of these things.

Soft inquiries are considered small talk at the beginning of meeting someone. Superficial and does not adversely affect whether or not they will go out with you. Soft inquiries can include men you may have dated or talked to but didn't sleep with such as meeting men on dating sites and letting them know how your experience has been so far with the site. These aren't generally viewed as being a negative thing. So, ladies, it is acceptable to soft-date multiple men (i.e., *The Bachelorette*).

Also, most men whom you meet on a dating site or know about dating apps are aware of the fact that it is a dating site to meet a potential mate and that you may be soft-dating multiple people. Your chances of finding a suitable partner for yourself can increase substantially by doing so. Some men won't like this because they feel like they aren't getting your full attention and that you aren't serious about them. A mature man won't. And unless you've been seeing him for a few months and things are progressing to that point, it wouldn't even matter. Also, don't be so quick to inherit a relationship out of loneliness. A man who is real quick to jump into a relationship might have other underlying issues that, if you aren't careful, can be unhealthy. I'd ask about his past relationships and how they ended. There could be a pattern there to be aware of.

If there were areas in your credit report that you could use some work on, you can do many different things for yourself to boost your dating worthiness. These include using self-help books and videos, getting a life coach, getting counseling, meditating, getting a better education, learning to love yourself, not being so needy, fixing your trust issues, forgiving your ex, not being bitter, enjoying life's experiences, or anything that will allow you to be a better version of yourself that involves *you* doing the work. When you feel you have improved, ask yourself these questions to assess your growth:

1. Are you free from past baggage that can hinder your being in a healthy relationship? This should mean that you aren't reacting negatively to past situations anymore.
2. Are you being realistic of the expectations you have on a potential mate—i.e., knowing he's not perfect or a mind reader?
3. Can you express yourself and your needs and listen to someone else's without being dramatic?
4. Do you have a positive outlook on life? Know that life is a series of experiences for your growth as a person.
5. Does your mentality allow you to work through issues without treating them like the end of the relationship but as a discussion, without being petty, childish, or disrespectful (fight fair)?
6. Are you happy with who you are and not looking for anyone or anything outside yourself to fill a void?

7. Are you no longer needy or not in constant need of validation?

If you can answer *Yes* to these questions truthfully, then your dating experience will enhance significantly.

3
THE VALUE REALITY

Now you know what you are eligible for as far as your creditworthiness is concerned and whether or not you should even be dating. Now you have to determine what you want and what you're looking for in a potential vehicle (man). Before you go dating or purchasing a car, you should do your research long before you set foot in a dealership. This is the credit report/repair part. *Do not skip this step!* It is vital to your car-buying (dating) experience.

First, figure out what you want in the car. Do you want it because you need it for work? Do you have one but want another one just to make you look good when you go out? This is where you can compile your list of expectations for the type of car (man) you want to buy. This can include color, make, model, options, and so forth. (In dating, this includes what he needs to have for you to consider him a viable candidate to date.)

As women, you tend to go for what is going to make you look good—the cute car, the car that says, "This is who

I am!" Basically, with men, you want a man to look good and for others to think he looks good and you want him to increase your status and give you beautiful offspring. These are things that have nothing to do with the purpose of the car (man). It's all superficial and selfish. Dating with this mind-set will surely establish a pattern of failure in any healthy relationship. You fall in this category if your requirements include any of these: finances; looks; type of job, house, or car; or who he knows. These things are about a man's lifestyle, not about the man himself or his character.

If you're dating to improve your lifestyle, then yes, you should include those things. But if you are in search of a life partner, then you need to delve deeper into things he should have *in* him and not things he *possesses*. Some things to include if they're not already on your list are the following: someone who will respect you (is he mindful of your feelings and thoughts?), someone who treats you like you matter (he makes you his priority.), someone who is supportive (does he encourage your dreams and ambitions or participate in them with you?), or someone you can grow with (can you build with him or make each other better without it being a competition?). In car buying, this would be looking for the most dependable and reliable car with better longevity in terms of use.

Looking to date a man with your unrealistic list of demands mostly based on your ego, on what you want and not necessarily what you need, makes the pool from which this kind of man you are searching for very small, and the odds of you finding this man dramatically decreases. As much as you are told about your worth—and by no means am I telling you to lower your standards on what you believe you deserve or how you value your worthiness—you should use that in the proper context for dating. This manual simply shows you how your concept of worthiness could be flawed or unrealistic in the realm of dating.

Women have elevated themselves with their independence—so much so that the dependency on men has all but become as needed for companionship. This logic would have one think that they have a high value and therefore worthiness of becoming the unicorn. This is a flawed concept to a degree. Hear me out. Lots of women around you and with whom you may have networked would qualify (according to accepted standards) as a good woman (cooks, cleans, good sex, educated, and independent). That puts most women in a very large pool of potential wifey material for a quality man. Now the problem lies with the amount of quality men (financially secure, stable lifestyle, mentally mature, respectful, compassionate, and wants to be in a relationship) that are available. This fact alone increases a quality man's value and lessens (not cheapens) that of a quality woman. Let's consider the car-buying perspective.

As a woman, you have your value system of what you think of as your worth. You were shown in the second chapter how to properly assess your worthiness. Even so, if you pull your credit score (based on what you believe and what others have told you), and it tells you, you have an 800+ score, you feel like you are ready to go get that car (man). So you go shopping, thinking that you're in a good position to be able to get anything that you are looking for.

Now keep in mind that the dealership's (potential mates') credit report search is different in terms of requirements like utility companies and may not reflect what you think your worth is because their focus is different on credit worthiness. Though you believe that you are an 800, after talking and spending time with you and seeing how you handle different situations, the dealership (man) may come back with a score of 600+, and therefore you don't qualify for that quality vehicle (man) you thought you did.

Knowing that this is a quality dealership (man)—i.e. Mercedes, Porsche, Lamborghini—they aren't known for having to negotiate their value. You know it's quality and understand the cost associated with this quality. Now, here is the bad news: he knows you want him (car), but he also knows that you don't qualify as a wife for him. But men have multiple positions that can be filled in their life. He may accept your offer, or he may offer you something lesser, and you may still get him, somewhat.

THE CARFACTS OF DATING!

In dating, this is when you realize that you're only qualified to be Friends with Benefits or find yourself in a "Situationship" or that you don't have a chance to ever level up in the relationship. You still got the car (man) but not the level of service you would have received if he didn't lower your score based on what he discovered about you. Many women will settle for this or spend more time, energy, and effort trying to convince them that you are qualified for this man just for you to get the vehicle (man). Some women get surgery or wear so much makeup that they look like someone else, they compromise themselves by putting up with things they said they wouldn't, just to be with him or to get him. Like paying a higher annual percentage rate (APR) than necessary just to get with him.

You could have gone with a more reliable car (man) that will be there for the long haul without costing you a liver, but you just wanted to say you got "that one" and ended up wasting valuable resources of yours on something that was more of a headache than it's worth.

Do you see how, again, you did not determine your worth? The dealer (man) determined it. Well, in the quality man's case, they are the consumers. So a man with a good credit score (quality man) shops, moves, and negotiates differently than women because he has a whole world of options from which to choose. There are more quality women looking to be in a relationship than there are quality men looking to be in a relationship.

So if you choose to walk away or not change your mindset to be with this quality man, he knows that there are fifty-plus other quality women just like you—or perhaps better—who are willing to accept his terms. That's why men visit multiple dealerships and shop around. And there's no sense of urgency for men to buy (commit to a relationship) because he doesn't fear the notion of "this one-of-a-kind deal will be gone soon!" If he doesn't invest in a relationship with you, there are plenty more women where you came from.

There is no fear in the quality man's car buying (dating) experience. There's more vehicles/supply (women) than consumers (men). So women in this scenario are the vehicles on the lot. The amount of dealerships on any one strip of road is ridiculous—many different lots with multiple brands and some of the same make and models but with different options—all with the basics of any working car like body, tires, engines, doors. This is the basic of being a good woman (cooks, clean, sex). *Basic*!

The options vary from DX, LX, EX, Limited Edition (education level, good personality, drama free, etc.). That's your value system in dating. You can believe you're the high-end store brand—and you may well be—and only for the high-end buyer. But keep in mind, you're the car not the consumer that is purchasing you. You want to be chosen and claimed in ownership, not the other way around.

THE CARFACTS OF DATING!

As stated before, the pool of men shopping at these dealerships and those who can afford the cost associated with purchasing a high-end vehicle are less than the average person purchasing a car. So be patient in knowing they are out there and willing to pay for you. Don't get frustrated seeing other cars taken off the market before you. Some men aren't that choosy and sometimes the base model is all they'll require and they keep them for the life of the car. Also, keep in mind that newer models are added to the lot every year, so don't place yourself so high that no one wants to pay the cost. Take depreciation into account too.

I hope this concept of worth is a better depiction of the reality of the dating situation.

4

Let's Go Shopping Get the Carfax

You've received the information about how to improve yourself and make yourself the best possible candidate for dating. Now learn to better assess the man and his situation so you don't set yourself up for disappointment.

You as a woman feel you are worthy of or believe you are entitled to a certain lifestyle based on what you bring to the table and typically look for cars (men) that will make you look good to others. This is the fatal flaw of dating men. Finding a car that makes you look good is not at all bad, but be sure you look under the hood to see what kind of work may be needed or maintenance required *before* you commit to buying the car (getting involved with a man).

It has been common practice for women not to check the Carfax on cars (get to know the man) and simply take the vehicle (man) at face value and believe that the vehicle of their choice is in great shape. Not until you take ownership of the car do you find all the flaws within it. Knowing that there is a tool and a way to know what is going on with a man *before* you invest seems sensible.

The Carfax helps you take a closer look under the hood so that you can assess how well maintained or careless previous owners had been with the car (man) and how much work or maintenance has been done up to this point. The Carfax will indicate how well he's held up after damages or accidents caused by him or by others. It shows the extent of damage the car has endured, and how much maintenance it needs to undergo.

The Carfax is a detailed document, and every page and every detail it contains should be reviewed carefully. **Rushing this process can be costly!** Read and get all the information *before* making a decision on what kind of relationship you want with this car (man). This is the only way to assess whether or not you should invest in (getting involved with this man) a vehicle. The Carfax will give you information on previous owner history, title history, any additional history, any warranties, and a glossary. These are truths about a man.

Do not skim over this part!

In doing your research to obtain information from Carfax, the "Previous Owner" section is one of the first areas. Here you may ascertain how many serious relationships he may have had, if any, or the types of relationships that he had been involved in—that is, if he was a side dude, husband, father, boyfriend, or in a friends-with-benefits (FWB) kind of relationship. See what type of relationship he is interested in now. Is he a mover or runner? (Meaning, does he move from location to location or woman to woman frequently or is he settled, a.k.a., a serial monogamous?) You get this information by listening to him and asking him relevant questions, not just about his past relationships but about his life.

Observe his actions to ensure that they are lining up with what he's saying. People's patterns can be drawn off their early childhood and early adulthood traumas and life. It can help in understanding why they move and think the way they do. Learn as much as you can about his character, views in life, and his relationship goals while having fun and enjoying his company.

The next area is the Title History. This is important when you are trying to obtain ownership of this vehicle (man). You need to know if he is free and clear or if someone has a lien on the title of the car. How much baggage does he have? Is there baggage or baby mama drama? (Does his child's mother still have feelings for him, either good or bad, that can hamper the relationship?) Is he married (staying and playing), separated (in the house [trouble] or out of the house [potential])? Or does he have a live-in girlfriend he claims is a roommate which is why you can't come by or stay over? These are important things to know when you are getting to know or purchase a vehicle (man).

These can be potential issues because that means the title isn't free and clear!

Be prepared to invest your time in trying to get these cleared or chalk this up as a lemon for you and avoid the headache. Just like the history part of your credit report is what he uses to ascertain if you are viable to date. His history should also be used to determine the potential and/or red flags of bad patterns to which you should be paying attention and using as your tool to assess whether or not he's compatible with you.

The additional history covers any structural damage (what's his temper like when dealing with situations), accidents (wounded by past lover and didn't heal, meaning he's emotionally unavailable to you), or if he is controlling (tells you what to wear, how to style your hair, picks or controls who your friends can be, or verbally abusive, calling you names or belittles you in front of others or alone, wants to know where you are all the time).

Getting a vehicle is cool and all, but having a lifetime warranty from bumper to bumper is even better. Be sure that you get the warranty you need, but better yet, be sure to read what you're getting. Check for the warranty offered on the vehicle (man). Most vehicles come with a basic warranty (protect and provide) for a specific amount of time in years. Warranties are up front for the basics; some other amenities may have to be negotiated. When you get the warranty, check it out and read it!

As women, we tend to think a warranty covers everything when in reality it doesn't, and we don't realize it until it's too late and an issue comes up and we end up having to come out of our pocket to cover something we thought was warranted and wasn't. (One example is when you're self-healing yourself after you stuck around too long, waiting for him to change how he treats you, when he said he didn't want a relationship with you but liked spending time with you.) Ladies, please read the warranty because you may not have bumper to bumper though the dealership may offer it.

Women sometimes forget that with all cars (men), maintenance is required in order to maintain the warranty. All too often we get so wrapped up in our lives and having a relationship how we want, that we forget to take care of the little things. We expect to get in the car and for it to start. We don't question how it starts or why it does what it does. We forget to put gas in it or get it washed. We leave that up to him to do and go about our day. Yes, men will fill your tank and wash your car not out of obligation but because they don't want to worry about you being stranded somewhere and for you to have a clean car. Appreciation for those things keeps you from voiding your warranty of the vehicle.

You have to keep gas in it (feed him), get the oil changes (be open to new things and adventures), rotate the tires (change up the same sex), and give it a proper tune-up

THE CARFACTS OF DATING!

(encouragement and appreciation). Lack of maintenance can result in the loss of the warranty. The man will tell you what he is willing to do and not do and what he will put up with or not, if you take the time to get to know him. This is his warranty!

If he doesn't say it's something he will do, **don't expect it!** If it's something he says he doesn't like (lieing, cheating, drama), **don't do it!** Just because some car warranties cover multiple areas doesn't mean *your* vehicle (man) covers the same area... especially if you didn't ask for it to be included. *Be specific* in finding out what the warranty entails. Because failure to maintain the vehicle (man) within warranty will void the warranty and/or keep you from getting an extended warranty (continues the relationship, marriage, move to the next level, etc.) on the vehicle (man) later or not being able to use the vehicle for a while (the infamous "he needs space" cliche or he ends the relationship) or having to replace it altogether (he stops doing everything to force you to break up with him).

High-end cars (men) may require less maintenance, but when it does require maintenance, it may cost you more than you can afford in the long run. Calculate the cost and get the coverage that you need from the man's warranty. Ask for what you want and see if it is even possible to obtain from that vehicle (man). Because if he doesn't offer it, it's because he doesn't possess the skills or doesn't want to afford them to you. Any measure to obtain it will void the warranty and loss of vehicle. All men are not created equal!

The glossary defines what words mean to individuals. Just because something is said the same way doesn't mean it denotes the same thing. Also, just because you understand a thing as being defined one way doesn't mean it can't be interpreted in another way by others. You need to find out in the Carfax what things mean in regard to your buying needs. The Carfax is about *that* car, so make sure you understand the meaning of words spoken about *that* car and don't assume that everyone understands the meaning of things in the same way. Words like *exclusivity* to some means "commitment," while to others, it simply means "committed sexually but still able to date." Learn to look at and understand things from the man's perspective and not always from your own.

Side note: You can check the Carfax on multiple vehicles before buying or even test driving them. This is important in your dating experience. I can't reiterate this enough: it is advised to date multiple people like you would check out multiple cars before buying. How else would you know what you like or don't like or want or don't want, if you've never experienced true dating?! Some people just know, I get that. You hear the stories of a couple meeting and marrying a few weeks to months later and being together forever. That's great for them!

I, like most, wasn't that fortunate to know right off the bat. Now there are some obvious things you'll know, like you don't want to be physically or mentally abused or cheated on. For the rest of us, the reality is, we have to do the work.

5

CONCEPT AND EXPECTATIONS

This seems like sound information, but the problem is that women are terrible at buying cars. Ask any car salesperson—the easiest targets are women shopping alone. Why, you ask?

Well, first off, they know that the longer you keep a woman in the dealership, the better chance you have that she will buy into whatever you're selling and may spend more than needed on extras she never wanted or needed. Why? Because women don't want to feel like they've wasted the salesperson's time.

This concept is true about dating and why so many women don't enjoy their dating experience as much as men do. Women open up for dating, and when the first decent-looking man (women are visual creatures too) comes along—although he's selling something you don't want or not looking for—you hear him out. The longer you engage in talk or spend time with him, the more information he gathers about your preferences. He then tries to connect to you on something you just revealed to him, partly to make you feel like you have a connection when in fact all he wanted was to sell you a car and get paid or spend some time or have sex with you.

Now that's not true for all salesmen. Some actually enjoy their job and would want to create a situation that will have you come back again and again and not just for the quick sale. Nonetheless, this is probably the first dealership that the woman has gone to. And even though her thought was to visit other dealerships and shop around, this doesn't happen. This doesn't happen because she spent all that time with the one dealer who told her everything she wanted to hear about what he was selling and how his was better than anything else she could find, and he may have even convinced her to take the car for a test drive because he knows if she drives it, she'd be more inclined to keep it. So against her better judgment, she test drives the car.

It may or may not feel good for her or it may not be quite what she was looking for (a family vehicle but convinced to buy a two-seater with a letdown second-row seat), but because she test drove it (don't want to feel or look like a hoe), she feels obligated to ride it out, instead of taking her time, hearing him out, letting him know that she will take what he's offering into consideration but that she is still looking at other options. Of course, this will cause him to pressure her and offer her better. If it's what you wanted, then take the offer, even so, ask if you could have a couple of days to think the offer over and come back when tensions and emotions aren't so high. To gain some clarity on what it is you really want.

You don't have to commit because you test drove it. It may not have been a good fit for you, so why settle? She concludes that the salesperson seemed trustworthy based on nothing but words and feelings. Then a few weeks go by into the purchase and you're having buyer's remorse because you ran across another situation where the vehicle (man) you actually wanted came with a better deal than the one you got. But you committed so fast. You never even weighed any other options, afraid the one you had was going to go away and in desperation you jumped into the first relationship (out of fear) without knowing if you were compatible long term or not.

This is why more men take their time and aren't able to tell you what their intentions are for you up-front. They really don't know. *Hell*, you don't know until you spend some time with someone. That is the only way to determine compatibility with someone. This is also why men are more successful at reaching their dating goals, which isn't always commitment or marriage but the consistent time, attention, and sex from women.

Women refuse to date multiple men and vet them for compatibility. The first one who looks good and tells us what we want to hear—we give our time, energy, effort, and sex to just to find out he wasn't worthy of any it and then blame him for our choices and lack of actually doing the work to figure out compatibility long term. Nothing wrong with men using this method. It's smart and ensures that they're getting the best deal for what they want in a relationship.

Don't pigeonhole yourself to one person until you know he is right for you. Ladies, take notes from men. Take your time and get to know him over months before deciding to commit to a relationship or exclusivity.

Dating should be fun. Change your perspective on how you date. Think of it as a networking event or simply meeting new friends as opposed to finding your soul mate and life partner or a means to be in a relationship with someone. You put a lot of pressure on yourself dating like that—it takes away from the experience as a whole. You can't view a date that didn't end with another date as one more failed attempt at finding Mr. Right but one step closer to finding him.

Disappointment's main ingredient is expectation. Don't date for expectations—date for the experiences. Enjoy spending time with someone new and getting to learn something from them. Be present in the moment. Don't leap ahead no matter how good the date is (no mind-wandering how it would be with him). Treat him like a friend and simply enjoy his company. Let things happen organically and go with the flow.

There will be a time and place and a way to bring up real talk but not during a first date. Remember, if there's no vibe, that's cool. Hopefully you'll learn something from listening to your date or from any experiences they may have shared with you. If you did have a vibe and food and drinks were involved, then that's a win-win. Take it all in as an experience that you didn't expect anything from. If something does develop and you realize that you want to spend more time together, remember, **it doesn't mean he wants to be in a relationship with you**—only that he wants the opportunity to get to learn more about you. Remember in the definition of dating that the outcome may vary. Multiple dates is not a guarantee for a relationship. Keep in mind, it was only a moment.

Either way, continue to date others and be social. Meet other men because until you have the conversation (notice I didn't say *understanding*) about exclusivity, he is still just as single and available as you are. Be sure to have him define what the word *exclusivity* means to him in his words. Women tend to think because a word means something to them, it means the same for a man and then treats it like the truth. But it's based on our experiences. Get a clear understanding of words according to the one you're with.

THE CARFACTS OF DATING!

It will keep you from having many misunderstandings in dating.

Ladies, be cautious of those men who come and, after a week of knowing you, are ready for a relationship with you or say they want to marry you. Unless you spend every waking moment with this man, talking and getting to know each other, that doesn't mean he knows you well enough to make that kind of assessment. I know you would be flattered to hear a man say he found his wife and pull on your heartstrings, but get over the flattery and ask questions like

- What do you know about my life?
- What are my parents', siblings', and my middle name?
- Have you shared a deep dark secret with me that you wouldn't normally share with others (trust level)?

In his answers, always ask follow-up questions to understand what it means to him—words like *exclusivity*, *commitment*, and *love*. Ask what he likes about you and why. The *why* should be thoroughly explained without the generic "it's just something about you" BS. Ask *what* specifically it is about you that has him wanting to be with you. That will tell you the level of interest he has in you. Don't fall for the "I can't explain, but it's something special about you" bull. Someone who wants to be with you long term will take the time and be able to explain what you are to them and how they feel about you. Asking these questions early or getting the generic response means you need more time for him to find the words and actions to articulate those things.

Also, you need to be able to answer those same questions about him too. Men can read desperation in women. Women who don't know themselves or their worth are the targets, and men will run those games on women to get women to commit or have sex with them, and only then will their true intentions be revealed. Now they want to be honest about an ex that is still in the picture or he ghosts you (stops calling, texting, and dealing with you) after you had sex with him. So be cautious about men who want to be with you too fast. Revisit the Carfax section about his history to see if there is a pattern.

Ladies, knowing all that you know now, you have assessed yourself and should be in a good place to know what you want when buying a vehicle or being with a man, long term. But wait . . . there's more! Car buying on a short-term basis.

6

Buying for Convenience The Hooptie

I'm sure some women are thinking that after they did the credit check, they can't go to one of the big dealers and look for a car (man). Well, not every woman can afford to get a Mercedes or even wants one. For those women shopping on a smaller scale, you can still benefit from this dating guide. It's about understanding where you are and where you want to be. You don't have to *not* date because you haven't or can't get to your dating goals right now. You could be a work in progress, and everyone's needs are different. Knowing and understanding what dating realistically is and isn't will allow your dating experience to be whatever you decide is best for you. Know the rules and stay in your lane.

There are situations you may find yourself in during the dating process that are not ideal for you now, but if you accept what it is and handle your business accordingly, you will have a successful dating experience. You may find that your current dating situation is one that requires you to obtain a hooptie. Being in a "hooptie dating" experience is one wherein your current situation doesn't allow for you to be choosy. (You need to get to work, and he's got a car or he is willing to let you use one of his other cars and/or you need some bills paid because you didn't make some good financial decisions with your money.)

A Hooptie is someone that's not your ideal man (may not be cute) by your standards but reliable; not what you want but what you can use at the time (purposeful). He will require maintenance (usually sex, among other things), and you can generally get these with no credit check being performed or with bad and okay credit or with cash and comes with no warranty. Not ideal, but he's there and reliable at the moment—meaning, he gets you from point A to point B with minimal problems. He helps you out every now and then and has decent sex. This is a situation of convenience.

In other words, he is purposeful, and you may over time begin a relationship with him to maintain the consistent benefits you obtain from him at the time, even though it's not what you want and you aren't satisfied. Get what you need from your Hooptie, and when you're ready (you've gotten yourself together financially to not need a man for your mistakes), trade up to a vehicle (man) of your choice.

THE CARFACTS OF DATING!

Finding yourself in a hooptie dating situation isn't bad. This could potentially be someone you needed and would have overlooked and then realized that you are good with what you have and not go looking for something better.

The next sections may not sit well with most women, even though some are in these situations and playing the victim because they don't want to face the reality that they failed in the dating process with themselves and with the men they chose.

Please note that not all women want to be in a long-term, monogamous relationship; and it doesn't make them a hoe. Just like a woman who doesn't want to be a mother or wife, is any less of a woman. They just have different life goals that are in their best interest.

7

Rideshare The Uber Driver

There are some women who know what they want, and it's not to be in a relationship at all. They only want to enjoy the dating process and the company of multiple men. Like men, they are quality women and opt not to settle down and be someone's wife or girlfriend. They want to have the freedom to move and date how they please.

Every woman has the prerogative to choose whom she wants to give her time, attention, and sex. The fact that a lot of women won't, for fear of being labeled a hoe, is about those women. Those women who don't choose monogamy may choose to "Rideshare Date."

An Uber driver is someone who provides a ride for others. The job of the Uber driver is to come to you whenever they are available or as needed. They get you where you need to go and then go back to the business they were doing or find more people to service. When you sign up for this service, this is explained to you, and you have to agree to the terms before you can ask for services. Here is what you would label a friends-with-benefits situation or cut buddies or, in this setting, an Uber driver.

Note that you are not guaranteed to always get the same Uber driver when you want because he has other obligations. The problem lies when you only have one Uber driver. You will need to have more than one driver or you will create a situation for yourself that will get you caught up in your feelings.

When you spend a lot of time with only one person, you will tend to develop some kind of feelings for them. In "Uber driver" dating, you understand and the Uber driver understands you may have other Uber drivers who can service you; and no complications should arise from this knowledge, meaning he isn't going to stop servicing you. This is a situation where the guy won't care or ask what or who else you have been with because it's not his business anyway and vice versa. You are not in a relationship with him, and more than likely, he doesn't want one with you.

Don't confuse the moment. But keep in mind that just because he likes spending time with you, and talking to you, and sexing you, it doesn't add up to him wanting to be in a relationship with you. He still has other fares he is servicing when he's not with you, and they know the situation like you know what the situation is.

Do not get attached to the Uber Driver! It will ruin your dating experience. It's not their job to service just you. He knows it's not about him, like you should know it's not about you; unless you're actually together, just enjoy that moment. Again, it is *only a moment*. Take pleasure in it and move on. It will be healthier for you. If you want that kind of consistency in a vehicle (man), then *get your own* or have the conversation with him.

You now know what you are signing up for when you are Uber driver (friends-with-benefits) dating. Keep this perspective in mind when dealing with him, and you will have a pleasurable experience dating this type of man.

8

FOR THE SHORT TERM THE RENTAL

Cheating is a big issue and among the reasons why some women have trust issues with men. Cheating is a choice made by others or for others. I believe that some people cheat because that's just who they are, and I also believe that your partner can push you to want to cheat for lack of maintenance and tune-ups, voiding the warranty. Ultimately, it's still the cheater's choice. No judgments or opinions, but it's a preference for some.

Simply stating here the rules or guidelines if you choose to participate in this type of dating to get the best experience for you. You are the captain of your own ship, and you are the only one responsible for your choices in the end because only you have to deal with the consequences of your actions.

"Rental Car" dating involves married or attached men and one-night stands. Not everyone is willing or able to venture into the Rental Car dating" realm. I would suggest any first-timers to get your feet wet in "Uber driver" dating first before engaging into this pool. There is a certain level of emotional detachment and maturity that is needed to be able to properly navigate these waters. The faint of heart, those who fall in love and get attached after having sex easily, those who talk too much about their business, and those who have jealousy issues *should not* engage in Rental Car dating! A woman having these attributes isn't mature enough to be responsible for their emotions to be effective in this arena of dating and will not be successful at dating in this manner.

As you know with rentals, it's usually for short trips and not for an extended period of time over thirty days with accidents (with your insurance). Rental Car dating is when you're looking for something to drive for a short trip or to take for a spin but is mainly for recreational purposes only. Nothing more. In getting into Rental Car dating, one should understand the risks associated with driving someone else's vehicle, and that it can be very costly and comes with rules that you have to abide by. This is not for the faint of heart or the emotional clinger who falls in love with everyone soon as you have sex with them. This is a blood sport for the emotionally mature woman, because if you get attached, *you will get hurt*!

Maintain your own insurance (have other options) to cover yourself in the event of any damages caused by you.

THE CARFACTS OF DATING!

Don't make this your only option! Rental Car dating is not to be used as a rent-to-own or for you to build a relationship with. It's sex and fun and temporary companionship and then return him back to his owner if he has one.

Again, like the Uber driver, *do not get attached*. The rental may feel nice and you may look good in it and you handle it pretty good, but understand that you are only borrowing this vehicle (man) and you have to return it (him) to his owner. Failure to return the rental can result in penalties—worse, the cost to keep re-renting this vehicle can be costly and usually not worth the hassle, especially since it would be cheaper for you to just go get your own!

There are times when the rental car dating can become an "Uber driver dating" situation, based on the experience shared and the level of understanding involved. It still doesn't belong to you, but you have access to use it long term. This is like a corporate car that is assigned to. Know what you're signing up for and stick to the agreement—and don't invest anything more into it. You create your own drama when you deviate from the rules of this kind of dating. Be kind to yourself. Date wisely!

9

LONG-TERM OPTION THE LEASE

Now we all know that women are emotional creatures and will catch feelings over a guy quickly. These feelings cause a complication in the Rental Car agreement, which turns it into a Lease.

"Lease dating" is, of course, dating someone else's man (married or attached), even if it's only on the weekends and/or over a longer time period. Dating someone with ownership to someone else is what makes it a Lease. Now some women are knowingly leasing their boyfriends and husbands out, and other women aren't necessarily borrowing their man. (They know he's out there with other women, but they don't care because they are the main woman and their security means more to you than a faithful man/husband.)

Lease dating can be for those who fell in love with their rental and now want to lease it to see if they can keep it or those not quite sure if they want to commit to a vehicle (man) but want the consistency of a maintenance man that you think (or know) is only servicing one other woman (his wife/girlfriend). Therefore, you would not have the hassle of an Uber driver who may be servicing more women.

During the length of the Lease, you may decide that you want to buy it and keep it for your own. Ownership at the end of the lease is contingent on how well you took care of the Lease and the agreement that was established in the beginning. Violating terms of the Lease agreement will forfeit your option to buy, even though they may extend the duration of the lease for a couple more years. *Remember, it will never be yours to own!*

A Lease has more restrictions than a Rental Car. A Rental Car comes with unlimited miles (i.e., gets all their time for that weekend or until the next day on a one-night stand); whereas, a Lease has limited miles that can be put on it. Leases also have to return to the owner or dealer for services. Not *all* the time but every three thousand to five thousand miles (special occasions). This means that he is still servicing his wife—even if it's only on the anniversary or occasionally, especially if he's still living in the house. Rentals are short term, and Leases are rented out for longer periods of time like years.

The rules for having a Lease are, again, not for the faint of heart. Here are some rules to consider when thinking about a Lease, Lease-to-own, or long-term rentals and what countermeasures (insurances) you can take to protect yourself:

1. *Don't ask about the Significant other.* Frankly, if you cared that much, you wouldn't be sleeping with their spouse/boyfriend. Don't let them talk about them either. If they're unhappy with their situation, which they usually claim, they would change it or leave. Don't let them use your time to vent about a situation that they aren't going to change—it's wasteful. You can't get that time back.
2. *Get yourself an Uber driver.* Have a Second option because *he does*! As long as he is still in the house, that is *always* an option for him. Don't believe the lies! Keeps you from getting too attached. The lease/rental doesn't get to ask you about other vehicles (men) you drive or entertain. If asked, your response should be, "Not your business." If they say they need to know about it because of their situation, your response should be, "If you cared so much about your situation and wife or girlfriend, then stop cheating because that's the only way for you to protect her!" Besides he's not supposed to be sleeping with her anyway, according to him. So what's the issue? (Oh, he lied about not sleeping with her, LOL.) Use protection first and foremost!

THE CARFACTS OF DATING!

3. *Don't call the house to talk to the spouse/girlfriend.* Doing so shows you have failed the process and this dating style is not right for you. Again, don't care *now* about her knowing that you exist because he's not giving you what you want. You've been a secret for years! Keep that same energy for the duration of your lease.

4. *Don't speak to the spouse/girlfriend if they contact you!* You don't owe them an explanation of who you are or what you are to him—that's his responsibility. Direct them to the source of the issue, their man/boyfriend. You made no vow or promise to her; therefore, you don't address her or owe her an explanation. Anything she asks, you only respond with, "You need to take any issues you have with me up with your man," then hang up or walk away. Do *not* antagonize them either. It's petty, and you're better than that. Also, any other response may void your warranty or your option to buy later because you can't be trusted or loyal.

5. *Ask him to protect you the same way he wants you to protect him.* Discretion is necessary. Although you are not contacting the spouse, she may come to your job and put things out about you. She is his responsibility, and he should police her up and control the mess he created and protect you from it so you aren't contacted or hurt by the spouse in

any way. Remember, that what goes around, comes around. *Karma is a mean bitch!* How you got him could be how you lose him!

Leasing is just another option. It may be a good strategy for what you need at the time or it may seem like more of a hassle than necessary. It all depends on your needs. I wouldn't recommend more than three years on a lease. That's enough time to figure out what it is you want. If it's to further things with the lease, make that known at the two-year mark and see if there's an option to buy. If not, then any time spent after this is you wasting your own time. Do not blame him after this point or after you've spent five years holding out thinking he'll change his mind. Why would he? You're still there giving him everything he had before. Men are selfish. The whole thing about having his cake? Yep, slide that in right there.

Some lessors won't give you the option to buy but will extend you out another year (the promise of not now but later). If that year isn't full of movement toward you (i.e., moving out, filing divorce if already separated, paying off debt), then he's simply buying time and wasting yours. If you now want to go out and see if you can have a relationship with someone of your own (this is when dealing with someone whom you know isn't going or considering to leave their situation), then let the lessor know you're not renewing the lease and returning it because you are ready

THE CARFACTS OF DATING!

to own your own vehicle. After the two-year notification, you can use the third year to start withdrawal and getting back into the dating market. It is very unlikely that after three to four years that he will leave, and if he does, he is more than likely to want some time to not to be in a relationship, being he just got out of one.

Final Thoughts

Let's go over some of the main points of the book. Be sure to check your credit worthiness (know what you can afford). Be realistic with what you want (you won't get everything). Know your actual worth. Check the car's (the man's) history before you get absorbed in and consumed with things, not about its (his) character.

Be prepared to keep up the maintenance on the vehicle (man) of your choice. (This may require an attitude adjustment.) Work on having better communication skills and articulate what you want intelligently, without always having an emotional outburst. Listen to what *he* says he needs, not what *you* think most men want. Minimize the drama in your life and yourself. Do the work of finding out if the vehicle is right for you. Don't feel pressured to settle because you want to say you have someone.

Keep this manual close and refer back to it as necessary to help you understand the dating process of your choice. Take your time and enjoy the process without ruining yourself or your experience because of unrealistic expectations and putting the blame on men. A lot of what goes wrong—according to the dating code—is what you are doing to yourself or self-sabotage. You have more power and control in the dating process than you know, and you're giving it up by not dealing with reality and living in a fairytale world about what dating is supposed to look like, according to others. No one is the same, so don't look to others as a role model for your dating life.

Create what you want and walk proudly in what *you* have decided to do with it! The apotheosis of dating in this new style is you can now try approaching a man you find attractive instead of waiting and hoping he reads your mind and knows that you are interested in him. Afterward, ask relevant questions about his dating status. (Are you involved with anyone and if so how serious are you?) This will let you know his mindset on dating and what area you could use him in your chosen dating style and also to break the ice.

The chances that a man turns you away for being nice are low, but women fear rejection. Think of all the women men approach and those who reject them. They find a method that works and use it until it's no longer effective. Women want to be independent yet are still looking for a man to act and initiate everything. Then they get mad when a man doesn't pursue them the way they think they should be pursued, when he may not have known you had an interest in him because you were playing coy. Or you wonder why you're so fabulously independent and he decides that he doesn't want to be with you because, unlike you, he took his time to get to know you before he commits.

Equal rights and feminism would suggest that *you* can take control of your life, and in theory, you can do as men do—although most women won't because they don't have the thick skin required to deal with being labeled or there's this fear of being judged by what others think. Waiting on a man to find you lessens your chance of meeting that someone you may have liked because you never showed them you were interested. All the while, thinking that you can't be a lady if you approach a man. Independent much? Sounds cliché!

Now you have the tools you need to develop the dating situation that is right for you. Go out and have some fun! Dabble in the style that works best for you—be it a new or used, a hooptie, a rental, a rideshare man, or a lease. *You* decide which mode of transportation meets your needs. *Do the work* on you! Not only will it make you a better person, but it will also improve your life and that of those around you.

Appreciate others' company and the time that they share with you. It's a valuable commodity. Then you can sit back and relish the new life that you've created for yourself—*not* just your dating life but every aspect of your life!